SPIES!

T0101172

FEARLESS SPIES AND DARING DEEDS OF WORLD WAR II

BY REBECCA LANGSTON-GEORGE

Content Consultant:
Joseph Fitsanakis, PhD
Intelligence and National Security Studies Program
Coastal Carolina University

COMPASS POINT BOOKS
a capstone imprint

Compass Point Books are published by Capstone,
1710 Roe Crest Drive, North Mankato, Minnesota 56003
www.mycapstone.com

Library of Congress Cataloging-in-Publication Data
Names: Langston-George, Rebecca, author.
Title: Fearless spies and daring deeds of World War II /
by Rebecca Langston-George.
Description: North Mankato, Minnesota : Compass Point Books, an imprint of Capstone Press, [2017] |
Series: CPB grades 4—8. Spies! | Includes bibliographical references and index.
Identifiers: LCCN 2016031807 | ISBN 9780756555009 (library binding) | ISBN 9780756555047 (paperback)
| ISBN 9780756555085 (PDF) Subjects: LCSH: World War, 1939-1945—Secret service—Juvenile
literature. | Spies—Great Britain—Biography—Juvenile literature. | Spies—United States—Biography-
-Juvenile literature. | Spies—Germany—Biography—Juvenile literature. | Espionage—History—20th
century—Juvenile literature. | World War, 1939-1945—Biography—Juvenile literature.
Classification: LCC D810.S7 L295 2017 | DDC 940.54/850922—dc23

Editorial Credits
Megan Atwood, editor; Russell Griesmer, designer; Tracey Engel, media researcher;
Steve Walker, production specialist

Photo Credits
Alamy: INTERFOTO, 13, Sueddeutsche Zeitung Photo, 56; AP Photo, 26; Getty Images: Apic, 6,
Bettmann, 39, Bride Lane Library/Popperfoto, 21, Imagno, 49, IWM, 25, Mansell/Time Life Pictures,
43, Popperfoto, 9; Courtesy of the Federal Bureau of Investigations, 31; Library of Congress: 3c28525u,
35, LC_3c28524u, 32; Newscom: Everett Collection, 45, HEINRICH HOFFMANN/EPA, 54, KRT, 36,
picture-alliance/dpa, 46; Rex by Shutterstock/Len Cassingham/Daily Mail, 17; Shutterstock: ArtFamily,
cover (silhouette), BERNATSKAYA OXANA, cover and 1 (flames), Ensuper, design element, Everett
Historical, cover (cipher machine), Fedorov Oleksiy, design element, Freedom_Studio, design element,
Here, design element, Keith Tarrier, cover and 1 (planes), phokin, design element, Reddavebatcave,
design element, Shaun Jeffers, cover and 1 (buildings), SkillUp, design element, STILLFX, design
element, Vladitto, design element; Wikimedia: public domain, 18, 22

LC record available at https://lccn.loc.gov/2016031807

Printed and bound in the USA
080819   002559

TABLE OF CONTENTS

Germany was in a tough position after losing World War I. The country was forced to pay large sums of money to the victors, and its national boundaries were redrawn. This led to an economic depression in Germany that paved the way for a person with big promises. His campaign slogan was "freedom and bread" for everyone—what he had in mind was something quite different.

In 1933, Hitler was appointed chancellor of Germany. Soon after, he overturned the democratic system there to become the Führer, or absolute ruler, of Germany. He and his National Socialist German Workers' Party, known as Nazis, at first enjoyed broad support, both domestically and internationally. However, it wasn't long before the world learned the truth: Hitler hoped to take over most of Europe and create an "Aryan," or superior, race by wiping out minority populations. Hitler wanted to rid the world of Jewish people, Romas, homosexuals, the disabled, and others who did not fit his idea of perfection. Many in Europe and the United States became increasingly alarmed.

World War II started in Europe after Hitler's invasion of Poland on September 1, 1939. Two days later, Great Britain and France declared war on Germany. During the course of the war, more than 30 countries took sides. The two sides were called the Allies and the Axis. The Allies included Great Britain, France, the Soviet Union, and the United States. The Axis powers included Germany, Italy, and Japan.

The United States had sympathized with the Allies but stayed out of the war until Japan attacked Pearl Harbor in Hawaii on December 7, 1941. Japan had been trying to take over parts of Asia for many years, and the United States opposed their movements toward expanding. War felt imminent, but still, the attack on Pearl Harbor took the United States by surprise. About 3,500 Americans were wounded or killed during the attack.

In the spring of 1945, Germany's forces faced defeat. Hitler, knowing he had lost the war, committed suicide on April 30, 1945. On May 7, 1945, Germany surrendered to the Allies. Japan surrendered on September 2, 1945, after the U.S. military dropped atomic bombs on Hiroshima and Nagasaki.

More than 60 million soldiers and civilians died during the war. The actions of spies on both sides influenced and, in some cases, changed the course of the war. This book tells the stories of the daring deeds of some of these fearless spies.

Krystyna Skarbek, alias Christine Granville, was a fearless spy.

CHAPTER 1

Christine Granville: Britain's Beauty Queen Spy

As Count and Countess Skarbek of Poland leaned over their newborn's crib in 1908, they no doubt imagined a bright future for their little Krystyna. She would one day make her debut in Polish society, catch the eye of a young aristocrat, and raise children with royal titles.

But this was not to be. By the time she was a teen, the count and countess's spirited daughter was kicked out of one boarding school after another for not following rules. Krystyna attended Catholic schools and found the schools' required religious instruction boring. One time she even tried to liven up mass by setting the priest's robes on fire.

School wasn't all bad, though. Krystyna enjoyed sports and languages, especially French. Her athletic ability and knack for languages were to prove very useful in Krystyna's adult life. Around the time Krystyna's schoolgirl days ended so did her family's good fortune. The family bank went out of business and the Skarbeks were forced to sell their country estate. Worse, Count Skarbek deserted his family, leaving them to fend for themselves in the cramped city apartment to which they had to move.

Now in her 20s, and not the type of person to wait for someone to rescue her, Krystyna found a job at a car dealership to support herself. She also submitted her photograph to a local newspaper for the Miss Poland beauty contest. As a runner-up, she earned the title "Star of Beauty." But as beautiful as she was on the outside, her insides were becoming damaged from breathing the exhaust fumes at the car dealership. After taking X-rays, doctors warned that her lungs were permanently scarred. They suggested she needed clean mountain air to recuperate.

Krystyna found both clean air and a husband in Zakopane, a ski town. Jerzy Gizycki caught her as she tumbled in a skiing accident. Several years her senior, Jerzy worked for the Polish Foreign Office and was a world traveler.

VOLUNTEER SPY

In August 1939 Krystyna's husband was directed to open a consulate in the British Colony of Kenya. Jerzy and Krystyna packed up their belongings and traveled by ship to South Africa. From there, they would make the long drive north to Kenya. But within days of landing in Africa, they heard the devastating news that under Adolf Hitler's command, the German army had invaded Poland on September 1, 1939. Not long after, on September 17, the Soviet Army, in alliance with the Germans, invaded Poland as well.

On September 1, 1939, Germany invaded Poland.

As a result, not only would there be no Kenyan consulate, the future of Poland itself was unsure. Krystyna and Jerzy decided to go to Great Britain and volunteer to help with the war effort.

Within a few weeks of arriving in Britain, Krystyna found the offices for the British Secret Intelligence Services (SIS). She marched in and volunteered to spy behind enemy lines for the

Special Operations Executive (SOE). At first the SOE thought Krystyna Skarbek Gizycki might be crazy. Walk-ins often were, and her plan certainly sounded crazy. She had volunteered to ski from Hungary past the German patrol guarding the Polish border. Then, in occupied Poland, she would meet with members of the Polish Resistance and deliver and carry intelligence reports.

SOE intelligence officers were torn over whether to accept Krystyna's offer. She had the language skills, athletic ability, and personal contacts in Poland to be a valuable agent. But did she have the right temperament? Did she have the courage and intellect to succeed in the life-or-death stakes a spy would face? Krystyna's charm and fierce national pride eventually won them over. She was commissioned to be a spy for Britain, and was given the first in a string of several false identities. Her best-known identity was Christine Granville.

After a small amount of intelligence training, she boarded a train for Budapest, Hungary, to await orders to proceed. When the approval came to go forward, it was the dead of winter. Temperatures dipped to minus 22 degrees Fahrenheit (minus 30 degrees Celsius). Christine made contact with a professional skier aligned with the Resistance and arranged for him to act as her guide. The two of them boarded a train headed for Czechoslovakia.

DID YOU KNOW?

During World War II, the countries
involved aligned into two groups: the
Allies and the Axis. The Allies were at
first composed of France, Poland, and
Great Britain. Later the United States,
the Soviet Union, China, Canada,
Australia, New Zealand, Belgium, and
other countries joined.

The Axis side included Germany, Japan,
and Italy, with Bulgaria, Hungary,
Romania, and Thailand later joining.

They jumped out while the train was moving to avoid detection at the border checkpoint. They skied and hiked toward Poland for days. One night during a blizzard they slept in a hunting shack. Even above the howling blizzard they heard screaming but they could see nothing outside. The next morning Christine found two frozen bodies. They later learned that thirty Polish people had frozen to death near their hut that night trying to escape from the Germans.

After finally arriving in German-occupied Poland, Christine met with Resistance leaders. She brought them British propaganda to copy and distribute. Even as the Germans imposed their brutal domination over Poland, forcing Jewish people into ghettos and publicly executing dissenters, Christine organized underground radio broadcasts. She also collected information to send to Britain.

Each time she traveled she faced the danger of being searched. If the documents from the Polish Resistance were found, she would be executed, but Christine always had a plan. Once, the naturally friendly and attractive spy struck up a conversation with a German officer on a train. After cozying up to him she whispered that she was carrying a packet of black market tea for her sick mother. Could he be a dear and carry it for her? In this way she tricked more than one unsuspecting German soldier into carrying her documents for her.

FAST TALKER

She wasn't always so lucky. On one trip she and a member of the Polish Resistance were arrested at a train depot. The local police thought it was suspicious for her and her companion to be waiting at a deserted depot at night. As they were marched over a bridge toward Gestapo headquarters for questioning, the spies dropped their secret documents into the river below. Furious, the local police confiscated the rest of their belongings, including their ID cards. They discovered Christine's stash of money and had begun dividing it between them when they noticed her necklace. Though it was only glass, Christine pretended the necklace was made of diamonds and begged them not to take it. The greedy officers fought over it, allowing Christine and her companion to escape. Afterward, Christine's ID containing her "Miss Poland" photo was posted in every train station offering a reward for her capture.

In other ways, Christine's work became more dangerous than ever. Her home base in Hungary posed new dangers after the country sided with Germany in the war. As a result, Christine and another spy were arrested at Christine's apartment in Budapest on suspicion of spying. Christine endured two days of interrogation and beatings. Sick with the flu and exhausted, Christine devised a plan to trick them into letting her go. She coughed furiously and bit her tongue so it looked as though she had coughed up blood.

She claimed she was being treated for tuberculosis (TB), a highly contagious disease affecting the lungs. A doctor ordered an X-ray, and because her lungs had been scarred years ago from car exhaust fumes, it seemed she really did have TB. No one, including the Gestapo officers, wanted to get the disease, so they set her free along with her partner, whom they suspected might be carrying the disease as well. After Christine and her partner were sent back to her apartment, they escaped from Hungary.

With her cover blown in both Poland and Hungary, Christine was reassigned to Cairo. There she received additional spy training. She was eventually selected for one of the most

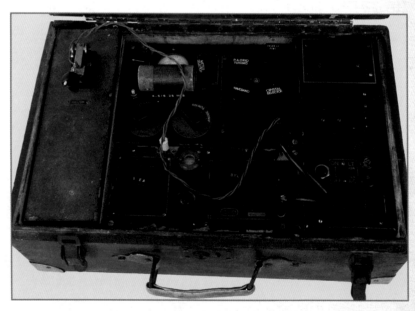

Christine used a radio like this one to transmit messages to the Allies.

dangerous World War II spy assignments: radio transmitter. The life expectancy of a radio transmitter behind enemy lines was six weeks. The woman Christine replaced had been captured, tortured, and executed. After training, Christine parachuted into occupied France in 1944 with a knife strapped to her thigh and a rubber-encased suicide pill sewn into her clothing.

Part of her new assignment was to work with fellow SOE agent Francis Cammaerts watching for midnight parachute drops from the Allies. They would race to pick up the dropped ammunition and supplies and then store them in Resistance safe houses.

After one run, Francis and two other spies were stopped by the Gestapo. Upon searching them, the German officers became suspicious when they realized all the spies' money had consecutive serial numbers. Consecutive serial numbers most likely meant they received the money from a central source, which made it look like counterfeit money. So, the Gestapo believed them to be spies. They were arrested and taken to a makeshift prison. Their execution was scheduled for three days later on August 17, 1944, at 9:00 p.m.

Christine biked 25 miles (40 kilometers) to the prison and slipped inside with visitors. She promised an officer there that she would bring him money if he arranged a meeting with the arresting officer. When she returned two days later with the cash, the Allied forces had arrived in France and were quickly advancing. It appeared the war was about to end.

When she finally met with the arresting officer, Christine broke the first rule of spying, just as she had broken rules in school. She admitted she was a British wireless transmitter. She pulled two broken transmitter crystals out of her pocket to prove it. Then she spun horrific stories of what the advancing Allies planned to do with captured Nazis. She convinced the officer that, since he was Belgian, his homeland would execute him as a traitor. Only by releasing her fellow spies could she guarantee his safety.

THE RESISTANCE

Resistance is the term used to describe a secret or underground group that opposes the rule forced on them. During World War II when France was occupied by Germany, the French Resistance, including a group known as the Maquis that Christine Granville worked with, did much to thwart Germany. Resistance members were often loosely organized, and their activities ranged from publishing propaganda, hiding supplies and spies, evacuating Jewish people, sabotaging enemy communications and supplies, and assassinating enemy forces.

Two hours before their scheduled execution, Francis and the other two spies walked out of prison, thanks to a rule-breaking beauty queen.

Francis Cammaerts (left) attended Christine's funeral.

Captain Ewen Montagu and his colleagues came up with the
idea behind Operation Mincemeat.

CHAPTER 2

WILLIAM MARTIN: OPERATION MINCEMEAT'S COOL SPY ON ICE

In April 1943, Major William Martin of the Royal Marines was dressed, packed, and prepared for his first and only spy mission. His job was to leak false information to the Germans. He had to convince them the Allies would land in Greece or the Italian island of Sardinia rather than their real target: Sicily. A large island located at off the tip of Italy, Sicily was an ideal landing spot for an invasion, but the Germans knew that and were already prepared for an Allied invasion there. If Martin's mission was successful, the Germans would divert their troops to Greece and Sardinia, leaving Sicily poorly defended. Then the Allies could land and launch a ground attack there.

Major Martin's assignment was a delicate one. He would have to be shipwrecked and captured by the enemy, allowing them to seize his false documents. He would have to play his part flawlessly. But even though it was Martin's first espionage assignment, he wasn't the least bit nervous. In fact, he had no feelings about the mission at all, as Major Martin was quite dead.

Major Martin was drafted into service by Captain Ewen Montagu and his colleagues at the British Special Operations Executive. The operation for which he was drafted was called Operation Mincemeat. Ian Fleming, an SOE agent and later the creator of the James Bond, 007 character, came up with the idea along with other creative SOE agents. They wanted to create the illusion that Major Martin was on a secret mission to deliver important papers when his military plane crashed and he was shipwrecked in the ocean. The SOE would make it look as though he had drowned and his body and briefcase floated ashore. It was certainly a plot worthy of a James Bond movie.

Montagu and his colleagues first had to convince their superiors the plan would work. Winston Churchill, the British prime minister, said they had "corkscrew minds," but ultimately they were given the go-ahead. Their biggest challenge lay in finding a dead body that no one would miss. And not just any body would do. The age had to be right for military service and the cause of death had to appear to be drowning. With some help from the local coroner they found an appropriate candidate. He was given the name Major William Martin because it was a common last name among British Royal Marines. Though many theories have sprung up about his real identity, it has never been officially revealed.

Ian Fleming, the creator of James Bond, helped conceive
Operation Mincemeat.

OPERATION GREIF

The Germans had a few tricks up their sleeves when it came to
imposters and disinformation too. They launched Operation
Greif in December of 1944. They selected German soldiers who
spoke English and dressed them in military uniforms belonging
to captured U.S. servicemen. The imposters infiltrated U.S.
units during the Battle of the Bulge and began causing chaos.
They moved traffic signs, destroyed ammunition, and cut

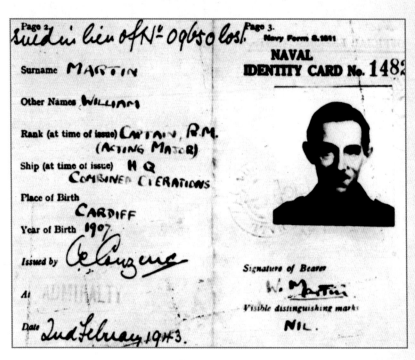

William Martin's identification papers

The SOE office created false identity papers and military records for Major Martin using photographs of an employee who resembled Martin. They carefully forged official-looking correspondence from one general to another hinting at the Allies' landing in Sardinia. These documents were to appear so important that the major had to deliver them personally in a briefcase chained to his wrist.

DID YOU KNOW?

Ian Fleming wasn't the only spy to write blockbuster spy novels. David John Moore Cornwell, better known by his pen name, John Le Carré, worked in British foreign intelligence during the Cold War. He wrote many best-selling spy books, including *The Spy Who Came in from the Cold* and *Tinker Tailor Soldier Spy*, which were later turned into movies.

POCKET LITTER

Worried that the Germans might figure out their scheme, Montagu's team had to make absolutely certain that their fake spy was believable. They created everyday items that spies call "pocket litter" for Martin to carry in his coat pocket and wallet to make him appear genuine: ticket stubs from a play, receipts, and money, as well as keys and matches. The major also carried love letters and a snapshot of his "fiancée" wearing a bathing suit. Montagu even made the documents appear worn out by rubbing them against his leg and folding and refolding them over and over.

The body was refrigerated until the operation started. Then it was wrapped in a blanket to avoid damage, placed in a metal tube filled with dry ice, and taken aboard a Royal Navy submarine. The briefcase with documents was looped through Major Martin's coat and attached to his wrist. A life preserver was strapped to his chest. An officer read the 39th Psalm and the crew prayed over Major Martin before committing his body to the sea. A damaged rubber dinghy was also dropped in the water off the coast of Spain under the cover of darkness on April 30, 1943. Spain was officially neutral, but its government was friendly toward Germany. The SOE believed any Spaniard who spotted a body in a British Naval uniform would report it to police, who would, in turn, report it to the Germans.

A Spanish fisherman near Huelva, Spain, spotted the body and alerted the police. Just as the British had predicted, Major Martin and his "secrets" were turned over to the Germans. After the Germans read the documents, they resealed them, placed them back in the briefcase, and the Spanish police turned Major Martin's body over to the British. He received a military funeral with full honors and was buried in Spain.

Meanwhile, the Germans couldn't believe their luck! They fell for the scheme and routed many of their troops and tanks to Sardinia and Greece to fight the Allies when they landed. But the Allies landed in Sicily, just as they had always planned, on July 10, 1943. With German forces stretched thin to cover Sardinia and Greece, the Allies faced much less resistance in Sicily owing to the work of an anonymous dead spy.

The Allies invaded Sicily, Italy, in 1943.

William Sebold (left) was a double-agent spy.

CHAPTER 3

WILLIAM SEBOLD: AMERICA'S NERVOUS BUT PATRIOTIC SPY

William Sebold was born a German, but later chose to become a U.S. citizen. Born in 1899 as Wilhelm Sebold, he fought for Germany in World War I, which led to injuries that would bother him throughout his life.

After the war, he wandered from one job to another and through several countries. He settled for a time in the Yorkville section of New York City, which was home to many German immigrants. He married the daughter of German immigrants and became a U.S. citizen in February 1936.

Nervous by nature and constantly sick with stomach problems from his exposure to mustard gas in the war, William required surgery to repair stomach ulcers. He and his wife separated during this time, leaving a weak and sick William all alone. Despite the fact that Germany was on the brink of another war, William returned there to recuperate at his mother's home in February 1939.

As required by law, when William arrived in Germany he reported to the passport office. He was interrogated about his activities in the United States and then told that the police would be in touch with him. A few months later, a man named Dr. Gassner showed up at his mother's house. Gassner said the Germans wanted him to work for them when he returned to America. William wasn't interested, but Gassner threatened to report that William had lied on his American citizenship application, failing to reveal his time served in a German jail. Gassner gave him a month to decide. Fearing for both his life and his mother's life if he refused, Sebold agreed, even while his loyalty lay with America.

William was trained to send messages using Morse code and a coding system using pages from a popular novel. He learned about microphotography and microdots, which shrank pictures and words, making them visible only with a magnifying lens.

While William was in Germany, his American passport was stolen. He reported it to the U.S. consulate and took the opportunity to tell the staff he had been blackmailed into spying for the Germans, but was loyal to the United States. Could the United States help him? U.S. officials recorded his information but were skeptical.

William continued his German spy training with a heavy heart. After a brief hospitalization for his nerves, the Germans gave him U.S. currency and names of contacts in the United States. They ordered him to purchase a special camera for microphotography and a radio device to send and receive transmissions once he was back in America. They gave him a code name—Harry Sawyer—and sent him to New York.

AMERICAN SPY

With his new marching orders, William was sent back to his adopted American homeland aboard the USS *Washington* in February 1940. When he arrived in America, two Federal Bureau of Investigation (FBI) agents met him. It was the first sign William had that his request at the consulate had been taken seriously. The FBI offered him a job as a double agent at a salary of $50 a month.

The FBI set up radio transmitter equipment for William. They assigned an FBI agent to listen to the transmissions. William made contact with the names given to him while FBI agents listened. Before long a whole team of FBI agents were following German spies.

William's German spy duties included receiving packets of money from a contact who worked aboard a ship that made stops in both Germany and New York. William acted as the paymaster, using the money to pay some of his fellow German spies in the United States. Before long, travel between the countries became difficult because of the war, so a new method of payment was needed. His German handlers radioed a message directing William to set up a business where they could transfer money to him directly without arousing suspicion.

TRAPPING SPIES

The FBI was overjoyed—this would bring the German spies straight into their trap! They set up his business office in Times Square. The office of William G. Sebold, diesel engineer, was equipped with the latest hidden audio- and video-recording devices. The FBI set up its offices next door. Through a two-way mirror, they could watch and record William's meetings with his German spy network. Best of all, the Germans unknowingly footed the bill for it all.

Spies came and went from the Times Square office. Film rolled night and day. And hundreds of radio messages were received and sent. William, though generally nervous and panicky, did surprisingly well with the support of the FBI. It was the biggest operation in FBI history at the time. After several months of surveillance, the FBI arrested 33 men and women. Twenty-eight were born in Germany, of whom 22 had become naturalized American citizens. Others were from Latvia, France, and South Africa. The newspapers dubbed them the Duquesne Spy Ring, named for one of the better-known spies, Fritz Duquesne.

DID YOU KNOW?

Some of the spies in the Duquesne
Spy Ring were involved in industrial
espionage: spying on corporations
that provided the military with goods
and services. This allowed them to
photograph and report back on new or
improved weaponry, steal operation
manuals, and anticipate how many
weapons and goods the United States
would manufacture.

FRITZ DUQUESNE

Fritz Duquesne, for whom the Duquesne Spy Ring was named, had been a noted big game hunter in South Africa. He fought for the South African Republic against the British in the Second Boer War (1899–1902), where his life as a spy began. As a spy, he infiltrated the British army and posed as an officer to sabotage their missions. He spied for the Germans during both world wars. He tried unsuccessfully to assassinate British military commander Lord Horatio Herbert Kitchener. For this he was imprisoned in a British jail in Bermuda. He escaped and came to New York. In the United States he worked as an adventure journalist writing about safari hunting and even became President Theodore Roosevelt's shooting instructor. He then worked as a movie publicist for RKO Pictures and lectured about big game hunting.

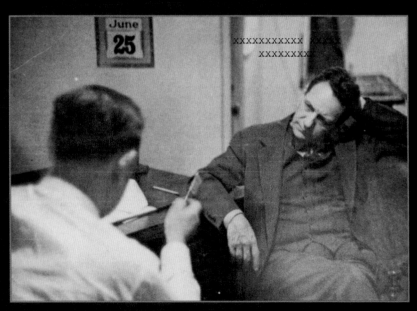

William Sebold (left) would have conversations with Duquesne and tape them for the FBI.

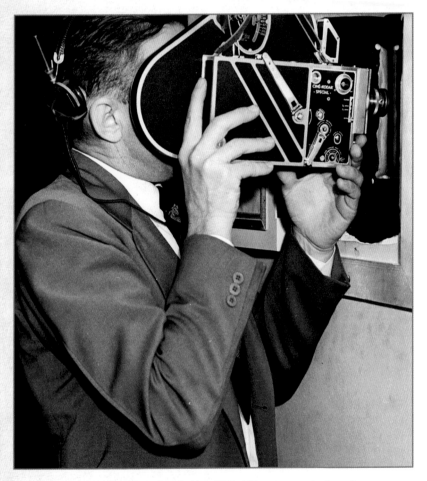

William Sebold helped the FBI film suspected spies.

Faced with the knowledge they had been followed and recorded, many of the spies pleaded guilty. The trial for the 14 who held out began in September 1941, with William Sebold as the star witness for the prosecution.

The events that took place during the three-month trial did little to benefit the defense. Although the United States had not yet entered World War II, their ships helped escort and protect other countries' ships. The USS *Reuben James* was torpedoed and sunk by German submarines on October 31, 1941, making it the first U.S. war casualty. Five weeks later, the Japanese bombed Pearl Harbor on December 7, 1941. Germany declared war on the United States on December 11, 1941. In return, the United States declared war on Japan December 8 and on Germany December 11.

On December 13, 1941, the jury deliberated until close to midnight before finding all the defendants guilty. They received sentences ranging from a few months to several years. William Sebold had taken down a huge German spy ring before the United States had even entered the war. In gratitude for his patriotic service, he was secretly relocated to Walnut Creek, California, outside San Francisco to start a new life, courtesy of the FBI.

PAUL BANTE — MAX BLANK — ALFRED E. BROKHOFF — HEINRICH CLAUSING — CONRADINE DOLD — FREDERICK DUQUESNE

RUDOLPH EBELING — RICHARD EICHENLAUB — HEINRICH CARL EILERS — PAUL FEHSE — EDMUND CARL HEINE — FELIX JAHNKE

GUSTAVE KAERCHER — JOSEF KLEIN — HARTWIG KLEISS — HERMAN LANG — EVELYN CLAYTON LEWIS — RENE EMANUEL MEZENEN

CARL REUPER — EVERETT ROEDER — PAUL SCHOLZ — GEORGE GOTTLOB SCHUH — ERWIN WILHELM SIEGLER — OSCAR STABLER

HEINRICH STADE — LILLY STEIN — FRANZ JOSEPH STIGLER — ERICK STRUNK — LEO WAALEN — ADOLF WALISCHEWSKI

ELSE WEUSTENFELD — AXEL WHEELER-HILL — BERTRAM W. ZENZINGER

**THE
33 CONVICTED MEMBERS
OF THE
DUQUESNE
SPY RING**

William helped expose the Duquesne Spy Ring.

Richard Sakakida, while stationed in the Philippines

CHAPTER 4

RICHARD SAKAKIDA: THE SPY WHO NEEDED HIS MOM'S PERMISSION

Born in Hawaii to Japanese immigrants, Richard Sakakida dreamed of life on the mainland beyond the Hawaiian Islands. He worked hard in high school, trained in the ROTC, and studied his mother's native tongue at Japanese language school in the afternoons. After graduation he worked two jobs, one at a furniture company and the other as an announcer at a Japanese language radio station. Each week he gave his earnings to his mother to help with family expenses. But Richard wanted more out of life.

When his former high school ROTC instructor arranged a job interview for him involving travel, Richard jumped at the chance. The interview lasted an entire day. He and 30 other young Japanese-American men were questioned by military officers and tested on their Japanese-to-English translation skills.

Richard Sakakida and Arthur Komori were both chosen for the job. It wasn't until after Richard accepted the job that he was informed he would be a special intelligence agent for the army's Counter Intelligence Corps (CIC). There was just one catch. In 1941 army recruits under the age of 21 had to have a parent's signature to enlist. Richard, then 20 years old, may be the only spy in history whose mother had to sign his permission slip.

Richard's dream of travel didn't unfold as he anticipated. He thought he would be taken to the U.S. mainland for intelligence training. Instead he and Komori were shipped to the Philippines. Richard's secret life began the day he boarded the ship. Though surrounded by other U.S. armed forces members also commissioned to serve in the Philippines, Richard wasn't allowed to speak to any of them so as not to blow his cover. He had to pose as a member of the ship's crew. When the ship docked, Richard was given a packet of information by one of the ship's officers telling him where to report.

Following orders, Richard parted ways with Komori and checked into the Japanese-owned Nishikawa hotel in Manila. He met his contact, Major Raymond, in front of city hall a few nights later. Given the code name Sixto Borja, he was told to check a post office box daily for directions. In order to gather intelligence on local Japanese businessmen suspected of gathering U.S. military information, he needed a cover. Pretending to be a Japanese citizen, he took a retail job at a store during the day. In the evenings he worked the desk at the Nishikawa hotel. This gave him access to the

Japanese guests' passports and personal information.

When Japan bombed Pearl Harbor in Richard's native Hawaii on December 7, 1941, it plunged the Philippines into turmoil. The Philippine government ordered all Japanese nationals in Manila to be interned at the Nippon Club, a social club for Japanese businessmen. Although Richard was only posing as a Japanese national, Major Raymond told him to keep his cover with the Japanese and gather intelligence. So Richard reported with his fellow hotel guests as directed. He stayed until two American intelligence agents got him out by posing as military police and pretending to arrest him.

Hours after bombing Pearl Harbor, the Japanese also bombed

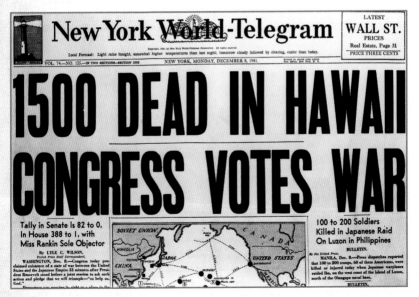

The Japanese bombing of Pearl Harbor on December 7, 1941, brought the United States into World War II.

U.S. military targets in the Philippines and soon invaded the area. As the Japanese army advanced, Richard had to stay ahead of them. He worked in Fort Santiago before moving to Bataan and then Corregidor, broadcasting American propaganda in Japanese, intercepting radio transmissions, translating enemy communications, and interrogating Japanese prisoners. He and Komori worked virtually around the clock, sleeping at their desks and living off ever-dwindling rations.

Shortly after Richard evacuated Bataan, it fell under Japanese control. More than 70,000 American and Filipino prisoners of war were forced to march many miles north to prison camps. Thousands died of injuries, starvation, and dysentery during the Bataan Death March. The island of Corregidor, to where Richard had relocated, couldn't hold out much longer. Richard and Komori were offered seats on an evacuation plane headed for Australia. But Richard gave his spot to another man and stayed to work as a translator for General Beebe and General Wainwright during the U.S. surrender of the island of Corregidor.

During surrender talks with the Japanese, Richard was introduced as a civilian translator, but the Japanese quickly identified him as the American voice on the radio. They would not allow him to translate for the United States. In retaliation for his lie, a Japanese officer punched him in the face and shattered his glasses. Richard wasn't able to see clearly again until after the war.

DID YOU KNOW?

In the years just before World War II, the
Philippines, an area of more than 7,000
islands, was under the command of the United
States. The United States operated several
military bases there, making it a tempting
target for Japanese aggression. The Japanese
battled against the Americans, Australians,
British, and Philippine nationals for control
of the area known as the South West Pacific
Theater. The area included the Philippines,
Dutch East Indies, Borneo, Australia, New
Guinea, and the Solomon Islands.

UNDER ARREST

Immediately following the surrender Richard was imprisoned by the Japanese, placed in a tiny cell, and given little to eat. Suspecting he was not only military, but in intelligence as well, they interrogated him around the clock for months. Richard insisted he was a civilian working as a translator. Although he was a U.S. citizen by birth, his Japanese captors charged him with treason, stating he was a dual citizen of both America and Japan, and was therefore a traitor to his Japanese homeland.

When interrogation didn't work, Richard was tortured day after day to confess. He was bound with rope and hung from the ceiling rafters until the bones in his arms and shoulders were dislocated. Despite being stripped and burned with cigarettes he never wavered from his story.

Eventually he was cleared of the treason charge when the Japanese discovered that although Mrs. Sakakida had originally registered her son as a dual citizen, she had renounced her son's Japanese citizenship before his twenty-first birthday. Richard lied to his captors, claiming his mother had done so because she had disowned him when he left Hawaii. In reality, she had probably been advised by his commanding officer to do so.

The Japanese captured prisoners and took them on
what came to be known as the Bataan Death March.

UNDERCOVER SPY ONCE MORE

With no confession, no treason charge, and no proof he was

military, the Japanese decided Richard was probably harmless. But

he possessed language skills they wanted to use, so they transferred

him to the personal service of Japanese Colonel Nishiharu. Richard

became his assistant and worked at his office. Before long he was

back to spying. He copied, logged, and filed incoming documents.

He now had access to valuable information, but no way to pass it

along to the U.S. military. He solved that problem when Mrs. Tupas, the wife of an imprisoned Filipino Resistance fighter named Ernest Tupas, came to the office seeking a pass to visit her husband in jail. Richard supplied her with a steady stream of stolen visitor passes and special authorizations to bring food packages into the prison. This allowed her to visit her husband and carry both Richard's messages and tools for a prison breakout.

During October 1943 Richard, along with members of the Filipino Resistance, dressed in Japanese uniforms, entered the Mantinlupa prison and disarmed the guards. Meanwhile, Ernest Tupas, who worked in the prison power plant, shut down the electrical system, allowing hundreds of political prisoners to escape. Once Tupas was on the outside he arranged telegraphs to U.S. General Douglas MacArthur's Australian headquarters, reporting Japanese troop movements and shipping information from Richard.

Despite having arranged the breakout of hundreds of Filipino prisoners, Richard remained a prisoner himself. As the war began to turn in the Americans' favor, Richard planned his escape. He hid pouches of rice, a mess kit, a knife, and even a stolen gun and ammunition. When the colonel and his staff evacuated, Richard claimed he was too ill to move, but would catch up with them.

He hid in the jungle, living on rice, jungle fruits, and grass. Japanese and American artillery shells rained down all around him. Richard was hit in the stomach with shrapnel and had to use a razor to cut the metal fragments out of his abdomen. Malnourished and delirious with infection from performing surgery on himself, he wandered the jungle for nearly five months. Overhearing two men speaking English, a frail, dazed Richard emerged from the jungle with his hands up. "Don't shoot. I'm an American!" he yelled.

The war had been over for weeks, with the Americans victorious. But before being taken to a hospital to recuperate, the young spy Richard Sakakida had unfinished business to attend to. Richard had to call his mother.

HIROO ONODA

Richard Sakakida wasn't the only spy to wander the Philippine jungle after the war ended. The world record probably goes to Hiroo Onoda. Onoda was a Japanese intelligence officer, who, near the end of the war, hid in the jungle. Upon hearing of Japan's defeat, Onoda decided it was a trick. For 29 years he lived in the jungle, eating berries and food he stole from nearby farmers. All the while he refused to believe Japan had lost the war. Finally, in 1974, he came out of hiding. Dressed in his ragged military uniform, Onoda presented his sword to his former commanding officer. He returned to Japan as a hero.

Hiroo Onoda refused to believe that Japan surrendered.

Claus Schenk Graf von Stauffenberg,
plotted against Hitler.

CHAPTER 5

Claus Schenk Graf von Stauffenberg: Operation Valkyrie's Three-Fingered Spy

Count Alfred von Stauffenberg did not think his youngest son's decision to join the Cavalry Regiment of the German army in April 1926, was a wise choice. A career in the army was so beneath him, so lower-class. Men did not make a name for themselves in the army. Before the German Revolution of 1918, which had abolished royal rule and noble titles, the elder von Stauffenberg had served the king of Wurttemberg (an area of old Germany) as Lord Chamberlain. Little did the count know that his son's name would one day be infamous.

Claus did well in the army. He was an excellent horseman, proud German, and quick thinker. In 1936 he graduated from cavalry horses to tanks and motorcycles in the elite Berlin War Academy. There he met other young men from aristocratic families in a group called the Kreisau Circle. They discussed politics and ideals at their meetings. He was a rising star, first in his class, and moving steadily up the ladder of military success.

Though Claus was a patriotic German, he, like some other members of the Kreisau Circle, became disillusioned with Hitler's politics. Claus privately expressed disgust over the 1938 Kristallnacht, the Night of Broken Glass, in which Jewish-owned businesses were looted. Synagogues were burned, and thousands of Jewish men and boys were beaten, rounded up, and forced into concentration camps. Claus was a nationalist. He believed in Germany's right to wage war and wanted, above all, for Germany to be victorious. However, he hated the increasing brutality of the Nazi party. As the war progressed, he frequently questioned the tactical ability of the Führer, as Hitler was known. The Germans lost hundreds of thousands of soldiers in Stalingrad before finally surrendering the area on February 2, 1943. Claus von Stauffenberg knew then that something must be done about Adolf Hitler.

Claus was not alone in questioning his commander's ability. Several members of the army shared his views, including some of his old friends from the Kreisau Circle. But Claus had little time for such thoughts. He was sent to the African front to serve in Tunis, Tunisia the same month, February 1943. Two months later, on April 7, Claus's vehicle was hit by American bombers. Claus lost his left eye and had his right hand amputated as well as two fingers from his left hand. For the rest of his life he wore an eye patch and had only three, badly scarred, fingers.

Adolf Hitler (center), Führer of Germany,
started World War II.

PLOTTER

It was while he was recuperating that Claus von Stauffenberg's

life took a sudden turn. General Olbricht, head of the General

Army Office, appointed Claus his new chief of staff. To choose

a seriously wounded man for such an important office may have

raised some eyebrows. But Olbricht saw in Claus the two qualities

he most wanted in his staff: a love of Germany and a hatred of

Adolf Hitler. Claus von Stauffenberg had stepped into an inner circle of army leaders that included Hans Oster and Henning von Tresckow from the Kreisau Circle. Both had already tried unsuccessfully to assassinate Hitler. Under their guidance, Claus von Stauffenberg became a spy, a plotter, and an assassin.

As the chief of staff under General Olbricht and General Friedrich Fromm, Claus had access to Hitler's schedule and was often present at meetings with the Führer. He and von Tresckow began plotting Operation Valkyrie, often referred to as the "July Plot." The real Operation Valkyrie was an officially approved plan to use the General Army to put down any planned revolts of foreign factory workers. But Claus and his fellow plotters used the term for their own plan. They plotted to kill Hitler, install members of the General Army in his place, and control the Schutzstaffel (SS). The SS was a militant group that served as Hitler's bodyguards and controlled the police and the gathering of intelligence.

The organizers knew killing Hitler would only open the door for other, equally unfit, leaders like Hermann Göring or Heinrich Himmler to take his spot. The conspirators planned to either assassinate them at the same time or immediately after they killed Hitler. They prepared lists of names to take over government positions. Even the announcement of the Führer's death was planned ahead of time. After bungled attempt upon bungled

DID YOU KNOW?

The word "Führer" is a German word for leader or, as it truly became known, dictator. The title became associated with Adolf Hitler when the German president and supreme commander of the country's armed forces Paul von Hindenburg died in 1934, leaving Hitler, then Chancellor of Germany, as self-proclaimed dictator and Führer.

attempt to get a bomb near Hitler, Claus realized being at Hitler's meetings put him in the best position to carry out the deed and plant a bomb himself.

WOULD-BE ASSASSIN

Carrying a bomb in his briefcase, Claus von Stauffenberg arrived for his July 11, 1944, meeting with Hitler only to be informed by one of his co-conspirators that Göring and Himmler were not present. They decided to wait for a better opportunity.

Their next attempt on July 15 proved no better. Whether it was due to Hitler shortening the meeting or the absence of Himmler, Claus did not detonate his bomb.

Discouraged by the setbacks, the Operation Valkyrie plotters met on July 19 to discuss their next move. Claus had been called

HENNING VON TRESCKOW

Henning von Tresckow, one of the Operation Valkyrie plotters, tried unsuccessfully himself to assassinate Hitler in March 1943. Von Tresckow asked a member of Hitler's staff to carry a package of brandy on board Hitler's plane and deliver it to a friend. Henning rigged the package with a fuse, but it didn't explode. Henning was forced to call the staff member and say he had given him the wrong package by mistake and switch the dud bomb for real bottles of brandy.

to a conference with Hitler scheduled for the next day. Spooked by the failure of their previous attempts, they went over their plan again, determined to succeed this time. After their meeting, Claus visited a church to pray, checked the bombs in his briefcase, and placed a phone call to his wife. However, the phone lines were down and he couldn't reach her.

Claus flew to the conference at Hitler's private hideaway, the Wolf's Lair, the morning of July 20, 1944. He was armed with two bombs in his briefcase. As it was a hot day, Claus asked permission to change his sweat-soaked shirt in a private room. One of his fellow plotters, Werner von Haeften, accompanied him, using the excuse that the one-handed colonel needed assistance changing clothes. Sweat dripping into his eyes, von Stauffenberg used a pair of pliers specially fitted for his three fingers to arm the first bomb.

He was interrupted by a phone call with a reminder the meeting was about to start. Claus knew Hitler didn't tolerate lateness. With only one bomb armed, Claus was out of time. As he walked toward the meeting room, a helpful officer, concerned for the one-handed Colonel von Stauffenberg, tried to help by taking his briefcase. Claus grabbed it back, but turned the man's pity to his advantage, asking that he seat him as close to Hitler as possible due to his hearing loss.

Claus sat three seats down from Hitler. It was 12:35 p.m. in the afternoon. He slid his briefcase under the heavy oak table as close to Hitler as he could reach. Minutes later he asked to be excused to make an urgent phone call. Once he was out of sight, he and von Haeften got in a car. Claus lit a cigarette with trembling fingers. Just as they passed through the security gate at 12:42 p.m., the bomb exploded.

Claus ordered his driver to take them to the airport. Hitler was no doubt dead. The conspirators would declare martial law and, as the heads of the General Army, take over power.

The Wolf's Lair was greatly damaged from the attempt on Hitler's life.

But at 1:30 p.m., one of the conspirators present at Wolf's Lair called General Olbricht. Wary of possible phone bugging, he said, "Something terrible has happened." After pausing he added, "The Führer is alive."

Hitler had scrambled out of the burned, shattered conference room with his hair singed, his right side burned, and his pants shredded. One of the conference attendees had been annoyed by the fact that Claus's briefcase was in his way and moved it farther away from Hitler. Four men died and two were seriously injured in the blast. Had Claus been able to arm both bombs, Hitler would certainly have been among the dead.

Returning to Olbricht's office, Claus heard that Hitler had survived the attack, but he insisted it was a lie. He had seen the explosion himself. They went to urge General Friedrich Fromm—commander of the Nazi regime's reserve forces—to enact martial law. But Fromm refused, asking how he could be certain Hitler was dead. When Claus replied, "I know because I placed the bomb myself," Fromm was horrified. He urged Claus to commit suicide. When he refused, Fromm announced that Claus was under arrest. Instead, the Valkyrie conspirators locked Fromm in an office.

The next few hours were a swirl of confusion as Claus and his fellow conspirators tried to take over the General Army and seize control from Hitler. The plotters called other units and issued orders to arrest Gestapo leaders and seize the communication

Friedrich Fromm stayed loyal to Hitler but was executed in 1945 anyway for failing to foil the assassination plot.

network, but their orders were met with doubt and fear. At 6:30 p.m., German radio stations broadcast an announcement that Adolf Hitler had survived a bomb blast unhurt. The Valkyrie conspirators continued to call members of the General Army, insisting the broadcast was a lie.

That evening a group of armed officers, suspicious of the phone calls and activity, showed up demanding to see General Fromm. The officers freed Fromm, who demanded the conspirators be put to death. Fromm allowed Olbricht to write a letter to his family. General Ludwig Beck requested, and was given, a pistol to commit suicide.

Just after midnight on July 21, 1944, the July Plot reached its resolution. General Friedrich Olbricht, Ritter Mertz von Quirnheim, Werner von Haeften, and Claus von Stauffenberg were lined up outside by the light of a truck's headlights and executed by a makeshift firing squad. Claus von Stauffenberg's last words as he died were, "Long live sacred Germany."

SIPPENHAFT

After the July 20 attack on him, Hitler instituted the practice of *sippenhaft*, or blood-guilt laws, to deter others from committing such crimes. Under sippenhaft, all relatives of someone convicted of a crime, or even suspected of a crime, could be punished or put to death along with the suspected criminal. Claus's wife, Nina, as well as his mother, brothers, uncles, and grandparents were taken to concentration camps. His children were sent to a special children's home for the families of so-called "traitors." Thousands of others, guilty by association with Operation Valkyrie's conspirators, were imprisoned under sippenhaft.

Timeline

February, 1939
William Sebold ordered to spy for Germany

September 1, 1939
Hitler invades Poland, sparking World War II

September 3, 1939
Britain, France, Australia, and New Zealand declare war on Germany

February, 1940
William Sebold arrives in the United States as a double agent

October 31, 1941
USS *Reuben James* torpedoed by Germans

December 7, 1941
Japanese bomb Pearl Harbor

December 8, 1941
Japanese bomb U.S. military targets in the Philippines; United States and Britain declare war on Japan

December 11, 1941
Germany declares war on the United States. United States declares war on Germany.

April 7, 1943
Claus von Stauffenberg injured in vehicle bombing

April 30, 1943
Major Martin committed to sea

July 9, 1943
Allies land in Sicily

July 20, 1944
Claus von Stauffenberg bombs the Wolf's Lair

July 21, 1944
Operation Valkyrie plotters executed

Summer, 1944
Richard and Filipino Resistance storm Mantinlupa Prison

August 17, 1944
Christine Granville helps free Francis Cammaerts on the day
of his scheduled execution

August 25, 1944
Allies liberate Paris

April 30, 1945
Hitler commits suicide

May 8, 1945
Allies declare victory in Europe (VE Day)

August 6, 1945
United States drops atomic bomb on Hiroshima, Japan

August 9, 1945
United States drops atomic bomb on Nagasaki, Japan

September 2, 1945
Allies declare victory in Japan (VJ Day), ending World War II

GLOSSARY

conspirators—people who plan to commit something, usually harmful or illegal, together

civilian—a person who is not part of the military

consecutive—in a row

consulate—a place where foreign officials conduct business

coroner—a medical professional who finds out how someone has died

counterintelligence—ways to stop an enemy from learning secrets

detonate—to go off or explode

disinformation—information that is wrong

dissenters—people who disagree, often publicly, with a position, person, or set of beliefs

dysentery—a disease that causes diarrhea and blood loss

Gestapo—the German secret police from 1933 to 1945

intelligence—when this is applied to spying, it means the information gathered during covert operations

interned—to be confined or kept away from others, often in times of war

Japanese national—someone born in and a citizen of Japan

martial law—when the military of a country suspends regular laws and takes over

Morse code—a system of communication that uses sounds or lights in patterns of short or long bursts to convey information

nationalist—a person loyal to their country, often believing their country is better than others

naturalized—having become a citizen of a country, in which one was not born

propaganda—materials, often misleading or exaggerated, designed to persuade people to join a certain cause or movement

skeptical—being doubtful or unbelieving

surveillance—the process of watching others

Additional Resources

FURTHER READING

Bearce, Stephanie. *World War II: Spies, Secret Missions, and Hidden Facts from World War II.* Top Secret Files. New York: Prufrock Press, 2014.

Hopkinson, Deborah. *Courage & Defiance: Stories of Spies, Saboteurs & Survivors in WWII.* New York: Scholastic Press, 2015.

Thompson, Ben. *Guts & Glory: World War II.* New York: Little Brown Books for Young Readers, 2016.

Throp, Claire. *Spies and Codebreakers.* North Mankato, Minn.: Capstone Press, 2015.

INTERNET SITES

Use FactHound to find Internet sites related to this book. All of the sites on FactHound have been researched by our staff.

Here's all you do:
Visit *www.facthound.com*

Type in this code: 9780756555009

CRITICAL THINKING USING THE COMMON CORE

1. How did Adolf Hitler come to power? What factors contributed to the nation of Germany following a ruthless dictator? (Key Ideas and Details)

2. Richard Sakakida had to get his mom's permission to be a spy at his age. Christine Granville walked into the British Secret Service and asked to be a part of clandestine efforts. What are the similarities in these two stories? (Craft and Structure).

3. What things did Ewen Montagu and his team do to make the persona of Major William Martin believable to the Germans? Cite evidence from the text. (Key Ideas and Details)

SOURCE NOTES

p. 45, line 4, Kiyosaki, Wayne S. *A Spy in their Midst. The World War II Struggle of a Japanese-American Hero: the Story of Richard Sakakida.* Maryland: Madison Books, 1995, p. 168.

p. 54, line 4, Jones, Nigel H. *Countdown to Valkyrie: The July Plot to Assassinate Hitler.* London: Frontline Books, 2008, p.197.

p. 54, line 19, Jones, Nigel H. *Countdown to Valkyrie: The July Plot to Assassinate Hitler.* London: Frontline Books, 2008, p. 209–210.

p. 56, line 14, Jones, Nigel H. *Countdown to Valkyrie: The July Plot to Assassinate Hitler.* London: Frontline Books, 2008, p. 235.

SELECT BIBLIOGRAPHY

Duffy, Peter. *Double Agent: The First Hero of World War II and How the FBI Outwitted and Destroyed a Nazi Spy Ring.* New York: Scribner, 2014.

Jones, Nigel H. *Countdown to Valkyrie: The July Plot to Assassinate Hitler.* London: Frontline Books, 2008.

Kiyosaki, Wayne S. *A Spy in their Midst. The World War II Struggle of a Japanese-American Hero: the Story of Richard Sakakida.* Maryland: Madison Books, 1995.

Kramarz, Joachim. *Stauffenberg, the Architect of the Famous July 20th Conspiracy to Assassinate Hitler.* New York: Macmillan, 1967.

Macintyre, Ben. *Operation Mincemeat.* New York: Harmony Books, 2010.

Montagu, Ewen. *The Man Who Never Was.* Philadelphia: Lippincott, 1954.

Mulley, Clare. *The Spy Who Loved: The Secrets and Lives of Christine Granville.* New York: St. Martin's Press, 2012.

Index

ABOUT THE AUTHOR

Rebecca Langston-George is the author of ten books including *Orphan Trains: Taking the Rails to a New Life*. When she's not writing she works as an elementary school teacher in California's Central Valley and volunteers as the assistant regional advisor for the Society of Children's Book Writers and Illustrators.